Partly in Riga

Also by Ian Davidson

Poetry
Into Thick Hair (Wild Honey, 2010)
Familiarity Breeds (Oystercatcher Press, 2008)
As if Only (Shearsman Books, 2007)
Dark Wires (with Zoe Skoulding) (West House Books, 2007)
No Way Back (West House Books, 2005)
At a Stretch (Shearsman Books, 2004)
Harsh (Spectacular Diseases, 2003)
Human Remains & Sudden Movements (West House Books, 2003)
Human to Begin With (Poetical Histories, 1991)
The Patrick Poems (Amra Imprint, 1991)
No Passage Landward (Open Township, 1989)
It Is Now as It Was Then (with John Muckle) (Mica Press/Actual Size, 1983)

Critical
Radical Spaces of Poetry (Palgrave Macmillan, 2010)
Ideas of Space in Contemporary Poetry (Palgrave Macmillan, 2007)

Ian Davidson

Partly in Riga
and other poems

Shearsman Books
Exeter

First published in the United Kingdom in 2010 by
Shearsman Books Ltd
58 Velwell Road
Exeter EX4 4LD

www.shearsman.com

ISBN 978-1-84861-130-6
First Edition

Copyright © 2010, Ian Davidson

The right of Ian Davidson to be identified as the author of this work
has been asserted by him in accordance with the
Copyrights, Designs and Patents Act of 1988.
All rights reserved.

Cover photo copyright © 2010, Ian Davidson
Author photo © 2010, Jemimah Kuhfeld.

Acknowledgements
Some of these poems have been appeared, or will appear, in the following publications:

Ars Poetica (Multilingual anthology), *Canting Academy* (Anthology IsPress)
Familiarity Breeds (Oystercatcher Press pamphlet), *Fragmente*
Karogs (in Latvian), *Poetry Review*, *Poetry Wales*
The Ground Aslant (anthology, ed. Harriet Tarlo, Shearsman Books, 2011)
My sincere thanks to the editors and translators.

Thanks to Janis Elsbergs for all his work translating my poems and prose fiction into Latvian, and all at the Latvian Literature Centre for their warm friendship and hospitality.

Thanks to Martin Solotruk and all at the Ars Poetica Festival in Bratislava. The poems in the 'Partly in Riga' section of this book were created as part of the Sealines Writers' Exchange Residency project organised by Literature Across Frontiers, with support from the Culture Programme of the European Union. My thanks as ever to colleagues and students in the School of English at Bangor University.

Contents

Partly in Riga

Dirty Money — The Riga Museum	11
Country Girl	12
Mass Graves	13
Café Cuba	14
Sunday Morning	15
Rumbula and Salaspils	18
Skulte and Saulkrasti	20
Occupation and Pre-Occupation	21
The Shopping Trip	27
Dear Diary	30

Wear and Tear

Wear and Tear	35
Hind Waters Breaking	37
The fuzzy world of felt	39
More morphine	40
A Mad Friday	41
Place of Birth — Theatre	42
Pods and Capsules	44
Roll Over	45
Brand me with hot irons	47
Poem about a dolphin	48

Partly Local

Cave Dwelling	51
Open and Shut	53
Don't fence me in	54
Ways around the Llŷn	55
Mother Fucker	59
Chalk Dust	62
Nasty Cough	64

Poor Relations
Poems through the politics of familiarity and poverty

No Go Areas	69
Count to ten	71
Stage Whisperer	73
Bird Call	74
Scared of Letting Go of Letting Go	75
Familiarity Breeds 1	77
Familiarity Breeds 2	78
the projectionist's tale	80
Fingers and Thumbs	82
Beach Head	83
Remarkable	85
Norfolk	88
Blackwater	90
Thick with History	92

The People Poems

Standing watching	95
He moved mountains	96
People 5	97
Trauma Unit	98
On a Station	99
People 8	100
The Day the Hell's Angels Came to Brightlingsea	101
Shop Talk	103
An announcement	104
People Again	105
The Scale of Love	106

This book is for Robert, Brendan and Gruffydd

Partly in Riga

Dirty Money — The Riga Museum

On the shores of Doles island the reindeer hunters
their situated pursuits; fishing, hunting, things
they can touch before the abstraction of coinage

and its brutal control by enforced amputation.
The scales that calculated the weight of
every crime that gets between teeth, scales

falling from my eyes. The insides of an animal,
the liver of a fish, is cleaner than
dirty money passed from hand to hand.

Failures of the Christian missionaries brought crusaders.
The same the world over, rock and a hard place, devil or

deep blue sea, Russia or Germany. Madonna on a
crescent moon waning the national awakening

Country Girl

Liquid cement poured down the gullet of a country girl
foaming at the mouth every opening stopped.
not knowing if she's coming or going. The violence
of the sex industry overlaid by a salacious aesthetic
concealing the enforced immigration of people not
even carrying their own passports.
The helplines are for the hopeless.
Get a gun.

Mass Graves

Nothing can prepare you for stumbling over mass graves. Between the birches, pines and rowans their raised lips indicators of the tumbled bodies falling from the crumbling edge into history. The shame of collaboration, of not being responsible of losing yourself to the system and giving it all up to the moment when the penetration of flesh is a simple response to an acculturated impulse of obeying orders.

Café Cuba

and I can only dream of moments and in retrospect
(the implications of our actions)
and the soft sound of the trainers on the street
(the waiting and the waiting for the end)
and no future left in Riga and the little that is past
(the flower pointing downward is a rose)
and it is tense in Café Cuba owing nothing
(and to no-one I was partly)
left in Riga with mojitos and the roses
(and a photograph of Castro on the wall)
the confusing science and rods of reinforcing
(and the obvious broken surface)
isolation in the moments I've left over
(and in the little time that's left for going)

Sunday Morning

Practising Rigan as
both a set of nouns and a method
of articulation he walked around
the place, from the parks that

encircle the old town
to the cobbled streets and the
docklands stacked with coal.
The thing with being strategically

positioned is everyone wants your
position. They all want to see the world
as you do. A tunnel opens out as a
system to be broken into at any point.

****

Waking early hearing a city
breathing. A blacked out Mercedes
slows down and then draws off quickly.

A cigarette arcs from an open window
lands on the pavement. A car alarm goes off.
It is Sunday although in Riga cloud cover is

intermittent. Someone is speaking Maltese on a
mobile phone. At the point of maximum curve,
stress fractures appear, points at which the

material begins to break up. Barriers tumble, one
by one; the early cigarette emotions barely in check
I could barely contain myself heart beating hard

half on the long sofa. Intellectual bullshit you smiled,
life is so much easier and harder than that and it's knowing
who you care about and where to put them in the story.

It looks like I can walk on water. Fuck it. These are hard
nights and days the split between mind and body is so
painful and to put emotions into a system as abstract as

language is too difficult. How arms so thin can even turn the
steering wheel, ankles support a body on twisting
stilettos. She ties back her hair, brushing it up from the nape

of her neck, squinting slightly into the car mirror. I could
ride the river rather than clinging to a rock as it rushes past.
With the tips of her fingers she smoothes cream

into her face goes to work expertly with eye liner.
It is a serious business, stopping to fix
your make up in Riga, and it is a serious matter to

sit in the margins and watch the street flow past.
Being a writer and bringing up a family
prepares you for almost anything. A foreign

city can feel much like home behind
closed doors and vice versa. We made
plans. They never came to fulfilment. My

self reflected and apparently tiny
beside the square jawed dummies
in their finery and with ivory fingers

that curve around my neck in a caress
that threatens the simple fact of the body
and relative prosperity kept at the

edge of consciousness. This was a
day job that was never enough. The politics
of the dress code and language that avoids the easy

flow of syntactical structure, alliteration, the coming
and going of punctuation. When words never mean
half of what they say and small hands clutch at something

passing by. You know the situation, a stand off between the
instant and its consequences. I sit and wait for some
time alone anticipating dialogue and its suggestive synthesis.

Voices, eyes glancing off the walls.

Rumbula and Salaspils

In a cold and empty place
standing on the edge of a two lane
road, women
flagging down cars before riding
off into the forest the
alien nature of space on an
inhuman scale and having
to run across the road and then
putting my hand out to stop
the bus or a hand on my arm.

The stand of birch where the
bodies were heaped up and
the crude symbolism of
naming statuary: the unbroken
the humiliated, protest, oath
rot-front, solidarity and mother.

The best get killed or fall
out of favour retreating to
their mass graves or holes
in the ground. I stroke skin
and think what little harm
it might bring. It quickly becomes
a battle ground between those
present and the absent,

the places themselves simply
sections of ground with a raised
edge for each mass grave. As
nothing and with arrangements
breaking like straw when the
body absents itself or is never
fully engaged then anything might
happen. The nature of admiration
and an inability not to respond.

Skulte and Saulkrasti

On the train line north of Riga. A line of
sand dunes topped with scots pine, birch and
rowan and a grey Baltic whipped into small
waves. What the fisherman in their small
inflatables saw as they stood around with their
backs to the wind much longer than was necessary
to discuss their catch. The left hand uncertain
as to what the right was doing
and just beyond their line of vision.
The next day thunder
rumbled in the background, rolling around the city,
the climate out of control
the heating boiler set to zero a heavy shower

forecast and all for nothing. We were wet, dripping,
leaking through the boundaries, hands breaking
through the surface of the sea cross hatched
and a line of waves breaking along the
shore. My back was a windbreak to fine
sand whipped up by a stiff breeze and a face
turned upward to a grey sky and a trawler turning to
show its length and the surface of the sea folding
over events as they unfolded as if nothing happened.

Occupation and Pre-Occupation

I have become preoccupied with the word occupation. It has filled me up and begun to control my everyday activities. I think about it, even when I am asleep. To be occupied is to never have idle hands. My preoccupation means there is no room for anything else. Every void has been filled. It's as if concrete has been poured through every opening in my body and then begun to set, foaming back up my throat and spilling out of my mouth.

The idea that words mean what they say, even on the inside (all the same under the skin). But then again a little of what you fancy and all that ... Occupy and vacate. Get in and get out before repatriation.

Without a clear relationship to my own culture I can't to talk to another. That's the easy way out, us and them. The consequence may be silence; gloom and preoccupation. Interrogating the landscape and other man-made artefacts.

my occupation of

my colonisation of

your every strand of hair

your every pore

I want to understand your reasoning

lock you up in my corner house

observe you from the corner of my eye

Latvia, you are my reason for waking in the morning
to check on all your occupations
my ocupãcija, my profesija

and if, in my examination of
hearts and minds, I should find a secret
then it's off to the woods, a blindfold
round your eyes, like the photographs
where Latvian women are stood on
the edge of a freshly dug grave high
heels clicking down the cobble roads
stonewashed denim showing the
occasional trace of blood and soil
the flap of low profile tyres on a
cobbled surface the hitch of the
micro skirt as I take up
residence in your brain

I have occupied the ground you stand on
taken up the time and
space that is the final occupation
of the multinational
of the industry of sexuality of the
never ending desire to consume

and produce, where the traces of consumption
are marked across the skin

there is little hard
evidence of that occupation
when we turn ourselves to symbols
of national identities, writers and
our networks of connections
class identity and a record of achievement
and all that is reflected back from the
sides of buildings is a foolish
overdressed sign of ourselves

there is no escape from the final occupation
it is always with us and has entered our hearts
our face and cheeks
the fluids across your skin
the worms of excess entering my ocupācija
my body reclaimed by the earth
fevered brain moulded in the
decline of the empire and part of your brain
and all the brains of official verse culture

poetry, my profesija, my obsession beyond

reason I talk to you and you understand every nuance

of my speech and every gesture. in movements

between the way I walk and a set of undeveloped

images. I work the streets, tempting people

into doorways from which they'll never emerge

unscathed. occupation cannot not have happened.

there is no way back. there are only openings

where you can be filled up once

more liquid dripping from an opening

the bullet breaking the surface of the skin

I am pre-occupied. you occupy me before I start

and running out from every finger sands of

feeling small electric impulses and irritations

that are partly pleasure partly pain. and all your

chains are velvet and all your words are

honeyed yet stick in the throat. this is not a

conscious act but the intertwining like

strands of silk as if your occupation of my

mind and body heart and soul is like the

repeated occupation of the Baltic states

is like my preoccupation with poetry

and my occupation as a poet.

under occupation your body

moves as it must move.

before invasion prepare yourself. sign

the treaty and print the early words that

will break the skin of culture. this is normal

that a country lifestyle could do with a little

nip and tuck and collagen inserted just

beneath the skin will plump up for

the kill. the poem begins to spread

outwards. by simple injections I

freeze the moments. wrinkles

that could lead to competing narratives

fade away and the working parts begin to rise

out of the frozen waste. I condemn other

parts to the ghetto, shutting them in

behind a high fence of language.

this is the final frontier. space and eastward

expansion into the Baltic. we will move beyond

Jurmala, past the displays of firm flesh

to a bright light where every wrinkle shows to

the flat bog where there is no hiding place

and to the white sands and the unmarked sea.

oh decoration there is no health in you if
I can classify a nation according to its
physical characteristics. I think. I think I can't.

and then the occupation of posture of
keeping her head on her neck and allowing
it to float above bare shoulders. girls
so thin and bouquets held with the flowers pointing
downwards the physical effort of maintaining
dignity on cobbled streets and our
invasive tendencies.
picking over stones best left
untouched. adopt a stance, look Latvia
straight in the eye as if I could determine my
own position by the way the world is reflected
in the surfaces and how I hold myself.

The Shopping Trip

1.

You were often disappointed
with the plastic olives
the pale over-priced tomatoes
and the moment between
the moments

Or the feeling of soft round arms
and olive skin
or cross legged
and at right angles
on a park bench
as an arrangement
of expectation
and delivery

2.

Hair up and then down
still and still morning

morning

a catch in the throat

at the end of the line
a pile of sand
between sea and land.

3.

Between sea and skin
pale arm
across pale sand

a vacant lot
a smile somewhere off in
the distance

4.

A failure to properly
turn out the light
the series of incomplete
endings
connections never
quite severed

Things coming in clumps
trying to take an
interest in my
surroundings,
trying to put the plug back in
as if language might become
something turned on
and off as if it doesn't
flow like breath
from an open mouth

5

It takes a heavy duty mechanism
to extract the juice and the pulp.

People are so much trouble.

6.

Over dressed and
clumsy, clumsy
pieces falling into place
in a public bar

Anyone could walk in,
the long ing at the end of
every verb,
dreaming,

Like a bell announcing
the entry of more flesh
and waiting to be rung,
and maybe untruths are

Finally
more satisfactory
however you fold the
timeline whatever

Bits touch together
there is no facility will
transcend the cancerous
multiplication of cells
poems growing like tumours

Dear Diary

Dear Diary On a gangway of a million shiny belt buckles; a conveyor belt going east. I am a travel agent; take off my uniform and try to imagine. There is only so much experience, the rest in the blocked out section beyond the tracks where vertical and horizontal combine until the place I'm in becomes a picture of the place I'm in. I've never been there and relationships may not be immediately evident.

Dear Diary Near the mouth of a river and up against the wall I learn to say certain words as a form of preparation. How much help will it be?

Dear Diary Your pages are stuck together with language like glue; they are plastered against the wall; a wall as tall as gravity permits in a surface that defies aspiration, sucking in the money. It is sticky with the heat of excitement and dripping onto the paving below.

Dear Diary I believe every word you say. Your handshake is dry and the words rustle as I walk through them, kicking them aside to reveal a pathway beneath, your skin has none of the usual signs of anxiety.

Dear Diary Melene from Strasbourg was an expert in Ai Kido and student of all things Japanese. I explained the principles of poetic composition to her. I was never good with girls. She asked me to write her haiku, I had forgotten how to count. She was a collector, her sketch book full of badly drawn faces of people she barely knew.

When we embraced briefly in the European way to say farewell at a railway station some miles from here, her skin was unfeasibly soft.

Dear Diary I am reduced to waveforms, patterns of sound and light. Verticals have become horizontal simply by tilting my head. The relationship of a city to the coast is not always immediate. Spat out of the mouth of the river an urban sprawl often spreads between banks. This one does.

Dear Diary My method is more than technique.

Dear Diary I believe in concrete. Where the con is the series of inner stresses that will blow it apart and a lack of integrity that bubbles across the surface.

Dear Diary I am impatient for you to fill, although I believe in you and your waiting page.

Dear Diary In the opera house I saw a ballet with the dancers dressed in army uniform. Or peasant outfits. They seemed satisfied with themselves and were very skilled, making fantastic shapes with their bodies. If there was a narrative it was either too subtle or too banal to follow. It was impossible to order a drink; the system was simply too complex. It was my first trip to the ballet.

Dear Diary Two men with a video camera approach a young couple kissing on a riverbank. They are asked to kiss while being filmed, and then leave with the two men. I express concern in various ways; verbally, visually.

Dear Diary The construction of a national identity is a violent matter, bringing wealth to the military men, the signwriters, cartographers, publishers and historians. The reconstruction of a nation is a homely matter; the books on the shelves, the food we eat, where we bury our dead and how long they live. Ancient pathways, brushed aside, distant feelings, it will come to no good, a temporary resting place on the road to all's well.

Dear Diary It's all due to dual coding. Separately and together. Deeper waters than I can possible imagine and repeatedly crossed by the disappearing tracks of ships as the naturalised relationships between language, landscape, and the in between.

Dear Diary I'm letting you down and engaging in other activities without telling you. I'm not keeping you up to date. Things are just moving too quickly and there is a catch in my throat.

Dear Diary I fear your manipulations. As I occupied you it is now you who occupy me. I am putting you to the sword, denying you the words. I am is nothing and has little to say in the order things appear—one after the other.

Dear Diary This came next. Then this. By rearranging letters from *diagram* I can make *mad* and *riga*.

Wear and Tear

Wear and Tear

The shape the fucking
Water makes and
The trackless seas
Or broken twig a
Torn square of material
Caught upon a
Thorn tree, bag
Of clothes in the corner
Of a room, upturned
Stone still damp.

Shush and go quickly
With little noise
Record only water
Passing, shush and go
The smoothness of
Stones, crushed shell
The wear and tear.

Or just brushing her hair
The shape the fucking
Hair makes held back
For applying make up
The familiarity of skin
Eyes after and afar
The shape the eyes make
Chiselled, drawn on.

The shape the fucking
Body makes and the
Thin linea nigra
The fucking shape
He's in, sticking now
In the tumble turns
Putting out an elbow
And the underwater
World he lives and
Makes shapes in
And wears and tears.

Hind Waters Breaking

Poked his fucking finger through or
A stray toe kicking at a section of
The amniotic fluid. Placenta still
Sounds like static and the fluid
Like wind through an empty
Desert or the movements of water
Deep below the surface.

He was an insider, with his head
Down. Trading blow for blow.
I drove south in search of more
Speed but was beaten to it.
No excess spilling from that sig
Nificance the car was sold.
Value lies outside of the

Representation of the event
In the gravel that the wheels
Kick up or the reduced
Differential its viscous
Couplings holding in the
Power or cushioning from the outside
World the bits that gush out or

Leak away as one more limb gets
Free from the pack or a leader gets
Promoted. There is no price to be
Put on life as capital does or any
Meaning. Broken free from the

Packaging a finger broken through,
Fluid trickling, meaning leaking away.

The fuzzy world of felt

These things that come to hand are never less than they are more their outer resonance and there were flowers there and birds and trees

All the cover that a runaway might use a well that swelled itself all day and every morning when the rain came

It was a world I made with tools that came to hand and neighbours ran as if their very life was up for grabs or only out of touch with everyday

Containing everything I thought of made a heap of all the picture cards arranged with images, peripheries patrolled to keep out key words or anything that

Might permit an order to emerge my widowmaker close to hand and all the little IEDs that make a march to falter or a country drive in someone else's country come on home

These things that make a world that changes daily from my window mountains sea and wavelets running all along the shore

Heart rate climbs and falls and his materiality becoming heavy slow and heavy as these things a test of nerve your resonance and foetal world of feet arranging

Oil and vinegar his hand to mouth takes hold of one foot and beyond control the pelvis still untested through whatever singing means I came and went

More Morphine

Something fills the spaces up a body leaves behind or when the desert mind is clean as bones still lying in the sand or when the world is stopping breathing

For a moment in an empty room the shuffling of feet could show me something of a friend and confidant a rush of blood

So where were we and whatever comes to hand with something of the immediate past and like a windfall or the heartbeat she was wired to

After an incision when they sucked out the all the water I have heard the beating of your heart I was the wind that's whistling through your head

I was the unused morphine in the corners of your mind and high on nothing much to do I lose my place forget my steps

A Mad Friday

(for Gruffydd on his birthday)

Breathing for the first time or tottering down an icy
Street on unaccustomed heels and off the shoulder

It is Mad Friday and Gruffydd finds his voice in the
Unused range of expressions. Morphine injections,

Salad dries out in the fridge. In the street someone
Pulls their skirt up to the waist while Gruffydd

Slumbered as in a hammock, happy in his world,
Its limitations expandable within limits until the

Knife cutting through the layers holding him by
The head and pulling, rocking to and fro until his body

Pulled from its learnt boundaries. It's a good day to
Expand your horizons and a day when you need to

Sever a long term relationship. Seek out new friendships.
Be careful of time wasters. Gruffydd yawns.

Someone shouts down from an open window while another
Points across the street or bangs the roof of my car. It is

Still Mad Friday and Gruffydd still yawning, waking up
His feet legs hands crossed over each other just touching.

Place of Birth: Theatre

'I was the father, it was a theatre'

Unsure of my lines having

Rehearsed for a different part

The men talked

Of the cost of Christmas

The way things go up and down

I was in the wings and

Dressed for the occasion

The uniform green and loosely fitted

While centre stage

Gruffydd entranced blinked slightly

His head long accustomed

To liquid a cigarette in one hand and ready to party

Head sore from banging bone on bone

Life became a series of snow flurries and an orange sunset

It's the equinox and the day is short

This too is normal,

The day ending in a burst of anger

Seeking out food for the untwisting

Seeking out the furthest reaches

Performance stretched to its limits

Pods and Capsules

The fucking pods man and a capsule.
Waiting as if to go off. And the cue
Cards were all colours so we took
Red last—emergency caesarian, back
Labour breech birth and the like.

I rustled the fucking paper. I spoke to Sion
Who had a blood phobia that
Kept him clear of the sticky end.
The roll call continues, 36 weeks, 38 weeks,
Bump envy, 41 weeks and still no show, the

Plug still tight in the cervix. The baby can be
Delivered into our custody before bathing and
provided with any drugs to lessen the pain.
Unused pethadin must be flushed down
The sink in the presence of the midwife,

It's that good. Any unused air returned for
Others to breathe any loss of
Feeling in the legs or pelvis returned after
Six hours. Go to birth in an egg. Signed
Another form, felt the fucking pod tighten.

Roll Over

(for Sue, of course)

I remember your loose joints rolling
At every movement across the axis, Sue
Turning and smiling temperature control
Off the radar turning and smiling
Lips never quite in shape, sincerely,
Never hot nor cold, jeans a little loose
Around your hips or corduroy worn smooth

I loosened the screws with impact
Prised off the drums
Marked the position of each spring
Removed the shoes
Mud and rust fell on my face
Brake fluid

I remember too your dark jeans
That accounts for you
The remains of the fire or
The burning embers
And a spark of recognition

My remembering fingers
As much as in your mouth
My memory in my mouth
Chewing gum and string
People and places putting

Our car back together reading
The hastily scribbled diagrams

He threw the car out of gear
And stamped on the brakes
The car veered violently to one side
The handbrake was useless
Fix the brakes he said and I did
Although the crank, loose in its
Bearing, wobbled as Sue
Loose in her bearings,
Travelled through blizzards
Her thumb high in the air

Limits of adhesion are quickly overcome, limbs
Falling apart or wear and tear
You turned up again rolled over loosely

Brand me with hot irons

A lighter held beneath nylon rope, hot and soft, twisting ends between his fingers.

He wedged the poker in the fire until the metal went a cherry red, and hot and soft.

They were never the same after, but grew up out of true,

Reproducing boxes full of junk and people never seen the same way twice.

Unspoken or withdrawn or cooling in the distance, engines clicking, tyres, brakes, the good cells say hello, roll over.

Poem about a Dolphin

Beneath shifting sands from Paradise to
Apocalypse under unruly hands and the patter of
Tiny feet a dolphin's beak emerged and ribcage
Out of where the wild winds blow from
The empty desert and the swirling storms of sand

Interference across a line of vision or the
Light smatter of a heartbeat between poles
Across the wall of sound stretched almost
To bursting beneath the shifting hands and feet
The swirling winds the dolphin disappears

PARTLY LOCAL

Cave Dwelling

For Kelvin and Melanie

The striations of a cliff face and its inhabited geometries a series of surfaces crumbling.

The cliff face falling away, skin burning under the sun, the surface of the country burnt away by wildfire, the sea endlessly shifting, changing colour, texture.

Stories eaten away to let in the humans, stories shored up a voice guiding you in, someone yells right.

On exiting it is left up to me to discover the difference between wanting to go, seeming to stay or shifting slightly, hair yellowing organs running counter to the idea of their construction.

Unimaginable and only describable in their own terms the holes appearing on the surface are also on the face of it and the source of their own destruction.

The prickly pear shot projectiles, it's soft she said and my hand became as a pincushion the holes became the surface you should sit in the caves she said and see it from the inside out.

I wanted to see things from the inside out without perspective; no words can carry nothing away; what can they carry?

Leaves, the word disappears and leaves a smile that flickers like a moth around a flame and like a scandal never put to bed.

Helicopters appear and a blackened landscape its roofs collapsed timbers falling in from the weight of themselves lives in ashes, apocalypse now flood and fire floating on a raft of incomprehension slow roasted kid.

The surface punctuated squashed out sideways falling away in layers to reveal, not the meaning but the caves.

Not holes in the cliff but places where people lived and had food and water lowered on a rope in a basket.

Dust falling from the corner of my eye on the soles of my feet from the cliff face the caves revealed to land at the foot of the cliff.

Dust wearing away and building up the crust of salt where the water has evaporated in the rock pools my skin turning to dust falling.

Coming down out of the hills and met by the sound of construction new foundations different drainage arrangements more electricity.

Language beyond a few phrases skin slowly thickening, browning, wildlife leaping towards the sea skin slowly burning pine trees flaring like roman candles.

The sound of building and the smell of burning off the surface off skin.

Open and Shut

Greece 2007

Fire spreads through the suburbs a thin voice echoes down the square two men leave a pick up. Two men leave a pick up and go into the woods scattering someone's ashes or fire lighters. The waiter would set out to cross the road without looking first and cars had to stop in time. Just in time two men got Tula out of her house to see the thin voiced woman after her beating and stood shifting one foot to the other as Tula readied herself. Quiet after the violence the afternoon sunbathers off for a swim a mimic acting out the voices the movements. The click of the electric going off the sound of the sea changing from the quiet lap of little waves to a roar of charred wood floating on the surface. The sun disappeared early into a wall of smog its colour angry its chorus the sound of helicopters the battering of pile drivers. The earth pounded by the pile drivers through the olive roots the roof clicking as it cooled the silence of the fire smoke rolling down the foothills. There were boats that sounded like helicopters, things misunderstood, electricity in fits and starts, the shutting of the gate

Don't fence me in
For John Clare and Blodwen

Gaze locked and teeth that show along the lip line, legs a parallelogram intense in its attention

Each occurrence of spring water a letter W for well across the surface of the map as paper wraps stone

She tries to dig the map while keeping to the high ground, grinning with cigar between her lips

Intolerant and inattentive, a collaboration of sheep 'Revolving their jaws with empty eyes' moving information

Through ruins of the War of Little English when a Lincoln man enclosed the common land

But Blodwen has him in her sights, gunning down intruders and burning up the houses that he built

And other marks that capital can make upon the landscape, the ruined houses on the shoreline of the lake the shapes of reclaimed land like Fen lands

On a little mountain a tribute stands to inoffensive poets and a view around the ruined castle of the Little English clearly visible and breached

By Blodwen who sits, smoking on a hilltop, teeth glinting eyes rolling, resisting enclosure

Ways around the Llŷn

Ways around the Llŷn, as in
Matters of unchanged names paths
To a mountain top to the start
Point of chequered fields and the
Precise position of objects.

Ways around the Llŷn only lead
To other ways around
Llŷn, places are near and far
As distance is, relative
And familiar to other

Parts of the Llŷn. Between first
Cousin and second the family
Farm is uchaf or isaf.
The ways around the Llŷn can
Lead to Hell's Mouth from easy

Pasture to open moorland,
Gazing down at Llŷn heavens
Open. The arch bridges of Llŷn.
The way to hell is neither
Broad nor straight but winds around

Its stops, pick up points,
Or opportunities,
Chances to change direction
Or disembark, holding up
Pale hands, signalling, gestures.

Llŷn has little room for idle
Pedestrians winding their
Way home under a low moon,
Revealing the route to Hell's
Teeth beneath the surging waters

Of the Sound that span around
Settling little. The Sound is
On the way to hell. The Sound
Is a heavy swell, the sound
Beneath waves is of a bell

Clanging or an empty
Vessel without love beneath
The hollow sound of an empty
Heart. The Sound swells in different
Directions the surface of the

Sound simultaneously
Peaks and troughs and, like a cork,
The Sound breaks on a rock my
Eardrums split a sound like an
Animal and like breathing.

On the landscaped surface
And on the way to anywhere,
Searching within ourselves for
Love in the Llŷn and overpriced
Parking, disinterested love

In the expensive fields.
Tired from the tramp of feet, blood
Singing in our ears from things outside
Things inside humming stuff
Stuff going on and coming

Off, blood, thicker than
Water inside the caverns of
A human heart its chambers
Washed by the morning tide
Scoured clean by the sound and every

Day the Llŷn cleaner the
Heart pumping with every upward
Step until blood, thicker than
Water across generations.
It was Easter and Passover

Or the fly past triple by
Pass or anyway my heart
Was surgically opened to
The wind around the headland
And uneven pathways leaning

Like a bent hawthorn arms at
Right angles. It appeared
Almost possible to fly
To transcend the cloudy
Sky, they are the politics

Of course of human love and
Best discovered at full tilt
And best forgotten in the
Effort to stay upright and
Best forgotten when recalled

In the night's Small Hours its
Little aches and pains the
Shape of the cross or almost
Ascension unobserved the
Teleport of G_d. It was

Easter so I walked the earth
Three long days skirting the
Jaw line of Hell's Mouth with its
Wet lips, the interactive earth
Where lights go off and on, the

Sun lays little eggs upon
The surface of the sea
And the chicks hatch chocolate.
Eggs melt in the mouth eyes water
In the wind the ways around Llŷn

That lead inward from leading
Outward from gazing down
And looking up from the dry
Surface of the earth in the
Rising wind and the high skies.

Mother Fucker

Dafydd ap Gwilym recited a poem of such merciless retaliation that Rhys Meigen fell a lifeless corpse upon the floor.

1.
Half witted bungler full of – faults
Clumsy, uncoordinated
Fucked-up at the good dogs
My feet popped out the good dogs

Dogs bark at him false lad – pup
Or text stuff on trees
Gratifying rub on tree
trunk hit the bing bong hard and

Bark at the dogs all gangly – nasty
Stinky lad, wandering dog
A fucking naturalist
And drinking a pure sing song

False Corrodian, justly – false me
Unjustly, is destitute
False and Emo, nor Norway
Or emperor or mother tongue

As false as the length of the – Teifi
The muscular Menai
Out scoring that tongue better
Be the best thing in your mouth

With words as fine as winker – edge
Of a wing as fine as
And false as the dog barking
The dwarf ageing and tongueing

Like a professional plumber – piped
As bitter song as worm
Wood and on the wing tip
Upstairs hard wood hammered home

2.

Words without shame gonna go – ape
I'm the wingman the guy
Always gets stuck with the ape
An imitator without

Thought processes his lifeless – words
Flattery without shame
Like who the hell voted for that
Shame or slept around shame of

Terminal disease so drop – dead
Indecencies backwards
Sinep or shame in her hair
Or I shamed all over her ass

Ugly blatant indecencies – flame
From house to house begging
'I heard you walking' for flour
Blatantly not amphetamine

Until you grind out you pass – out
Singing rock gull paddler
In an ebb tide cocaine or
Meth get a fat chick roll her

In flour and aim for the wet – spot
The size of a halfpenny
I'll have a lovely fuck penny
My halfpenny saddle ride out

3.

Would be a blessing to see him – swing
Dangly, nasty breeches, crooked weak
In the fine rules of metrics
Words out for themselves wear

Lippy and drunk on weak beer – puked
Chemically incon-
Venienced like a pirate
But more pain meat beggar dregs

Cockles you snog random then – woe
Drunker than fuck lukewarm water
Dancing like a girl's dad to
Cantankerous old songster

Chalk Dust

For Lee in Sussex

From profiteering principles
Turn to dust
Drifting like dandruff

Against slate mountains
Chalk cliffs
Wear away

Or across teaching methods a will
To learn and the ways of
Nation

There is only so much experience
The rest needs to be made up
Riding the lines in

Anxiety and with friction
Between the surfaces
Or no colonial construct

Is ever complete there will always be
Little words chalked up or
Alternatively spelt

And the worn sleeves of teachers
Who
In scratching away

May one day
Through flooded mines
Past deserted industry

Quarries filled with water the
Residue of coal, steel
Slate

Reduce difference to a thin
Coating that drifts in a thin wind
Trees, pit props, snapping like toothpicks

Nasty Cough

There was marsh
Under the surface
Pine trees
High in the wind
There were undercurrents
From hand to hand
Counter culture
Come into land
There was a heartbeat
Irregular
A lungful
Now and again
It was Friday

Week by week
Mile by mile
Fishermen
In empty lands
Staring out to sea
With empty hands
Share a fishing box
As a seat
Bodies joined
At the hip
Bay nearly silver
Creek by creek
Conditions tidal

From trawling
As B S would
Have it
Fishing out
Lame ducks
Things
Winched in
Stuck on the
Bottom pinned
To a rocky shelf
Sliding out of
Kilter tilted
Unexploded
Coughs rise
To the surface

POOR RELATIONS

Poems through the politics of familiarity and poverty.

No Go Areas

With the surface of the word unfolding new connections occur
Previously impossible to imagine from sites of special interest
Where the next body politic will come from throwing themselves
At the exhaust smothering the world in sound from their insane
Silencers and the baroque ornament of LED lights systems
And stick on spoilers. Silver track suits.

That bunch of middle class kids called new labour are little threat
To the established order or the self interest of the self interested.
The revolutionary sixties a parody of itself in the over confident
Long haired children spat upon by hard faced remnants of the
Industrial working class. Maybe the unions did more than we
Thought possible. Maybe stay at home mothers held

Communities together rather than working all hours to get a
roof over their heads in moments of property madness.
Maybe our imaginations cannot contain whatever comes
Next or reveal the language folded into the
Words where beginning and end curl upwards to conceal the
Filling. Maybe what is hidden is never less than and always

Something more. Maybe the sound of revolution is the alloy
Wheels turning and the residual kindness of community.
Better the curled lip of those that never have all the fruit and
Veg they need or mothers fit to cook them than the overstuffed
Vitamin laden smoothies laced with condescension.
Within the nominal optimism of Chavez lies the word Chav.

I hope he will turn out ok and not sell his soul. Wearing sports gear
And smoking is ironic in the ways inside and outside coincide,
Smoke curling around the lungs and feeding the blood ridden
Veins and starving the brain of oxygen its subversive status
Assured by its new found illegality. The future is unimagined
But cancerous, a dark continent shadowing the breathing and

Where the past is an insecure guide who often gets it wrong.
The new revolutionary guard are of both sexes and impossible
To articulate and therefore temporarily safe from assimilation
At least until their video diaries make the news and spell out
A future. They require a disinclination to play any system and lie
Outside common sense in the flickering nature of humanity

Revealed by every shift in position or new relationships formed
Out of a shifting gaze. It is the law of the father the girls and boys
Fiddling with the bodywork of their little hatchbacks and
Challenging any sense of structural integrity and then
Going out to spit on the students or pink tracksuits or
Hair pulled back until tears come or escaping representation.

Count to ten

There are snowflakes

Crystalline

One thing after another
One thing and another

Witness to change

Next witness

I came and I felt
This and that
As plainly as
The words allow

Power structures small voices
Relentless legal machinery
In the architecture of language
The voice of the recorder
The voice of the witness as if
To write it down
In the multiple systems unto
The end of the line

It's legal
Making it up
Blusher eye liner
Giving it lip

And stuck on you
Snow melting like mascara
After a hard nights sleep

And the unwanted attentions
That words can get you
When decorated
With intent
Or puffed up out of all recognition

Women tipped into the water
From the back of the boat that'll
Teach them or the family servant
Staked out and whipped
Blood drawn out in
That familiar way
A blood line from top to
Toe and in the family way

Uncommon speech laying
Out the way things are
The way things used to be
How you might turn out
The cut of your cloth
There are many sides
To the question
Asides, sotto voce
Snow softly falling
Crystalline
Obscure

Stage Whisperer

Critical infrastructure eyed up from face to face
the light in her eyes across a crowded room between
flash bulbs voice transmission a string of pearls.

Her manner was absolutely practical and could be
counted on. The others had some difficulty with the
everyday details, the unaccustomed plumbing.

Some demanded blood and as I am or extended
a single supporting arm to assist in the dismantling.
I failed to close the account. I opened a new page.

The set lists from too much attention so I go
back stage shore it all up with pit props examine
the staples rusting in the spine bent back on them

selves. Maybe it's all brand volume sales data and
these selves or this page, the art of thuggery and
other complex commodities. Speak in over tones

warn the others of oncoming storms look the storm
in the eye with a smile wait anxiously for the first
smile the glimmer of hope a stage whisperer.

Bird Call

Birdsong spitting on the street.
Over the hill dark clouds,
On the water, light. The
Agile pigeon flies along the

Platform chanting
To itself. Bulbs going
In the earth and
Other things unseen

Swelling as tubers
Underground where no birds sing
No birds fly. Sounds, a
phone, naturally anxiously

Bent over in order to
Hear against the tramp of feet
The bridge rhythmically a wall
Obviously the end of the road

Clearly coming into view or
Shortly the length of time
Measured off sounds off
In the distance calling me, calling.

Scared of letting go of letting go

Change is just a jingle in a rich man's pocket
And security a poor man's dollar (popular song)

I wear a blue suit and ride shotgun
Give them folding stuff to rustle
Coins to jingle in their pocket
I ride the dirty streets, go in the back way

Kicking discarded boxes, security light
And by myself again there is no shiny
Surface between us only the worn
Seats of cars the wrong side of reliable

And your thick hair between my hands.
My voice is thin and shakes under stress
This is no place for a voice without authority
There is no claim that can be staked

Bodies flare up, the brief moment of beauty, maybe
The bit between teeth the only bit I own
The words in my mouth expelled
With a breath maybe that's what I own

This bit of real estate
Stashed in the outskirts of town
An estate which is really real
That's the only bit of estate I

Own and then the houses go
From beneath my feet and falling backwards
Feet flying trying to connect with a foot as I
Fall backwards words flying out of my mouth

I had forgotten where the connections were
Or the electricity of class condescension where
Deaf and dumb with hatred welcome
To where the words have run out

And still scared of letting go of letting go
Of losing the simulation of freedom
The false consciousness of anything I like
The impossibility of an entire breath

Familiarity Breeds 1

The things that become familiar egret and red kite
The hesitant touch of children
Starlings flocking for bread on frozen soil
An increase in the crow population
Human habits remaindered
From when the earth was turned over

A harsh word in the wrong place and
Bickering endlessly and without feeling
Without value these things become familiar
Like boredom the sun, going down again,
that everything always changes, that this
Becomes familiar that things are always coming and going

I try to take up a position to fix a perspective
To line up the worn sight at the end of the barrel
With the slightly misshapen v the cracked stock
Pinching my skin and then staring into someone's
Eyes a bird flapping off and making the distance
Nearer the bird disappearing into your eyes your

Eyes taken up by the wings over and over flapping
In your head and circling, circling as if the rest
Between the beat of each wing might be the
Moment between movements the circling
In opposition to the ever onward in its repetition
A phrase that catches and again and again

Familiarity Breeds 2

The landscape is never normal
The land of my fathers
Home and on the range
Leaning after a hard day against the warmth
Roaming the fields in search of rabbit, hare etc

This is mother earth
These are my sisters, brothers etc
Circling restlessly the kite, kestrel and buzzard
A heron up to its feet in freezing water
Eyeing up a potential catch

This is the girl or boy next door
These are my neighbours
Moving from known behaviour to the unknown
From human to inhuman
From place to place

This is the food I eat
This is how I build my house
How I keep warm
The materials come easily hand-to-hand to mouth
I inhabit

These are the materials that I come to depend on
They are habit forming
The view from the coastline, fore and aft
A sight to see, before and after
This is the family, distributed in a series of nodes

But fatally weakened.
This is never normal as normal never is
It is an occasion a moment within
Moments a day at a time

And turning back to the way the road skirts the mountain
At the head of the valley or the long arm
Of a peninsula stretches into the sea or
The last leg or face to face.

The Projectionist's Tale

the crumbled remains of the empire
the demolition of the plaza
the domination of the multiplex

and maybe projective verse was written after
a liquid lunch with Frank O'Hara,
remote control to hand, switching channels
on the flat reflective surfaces of the TV
lit from behind and from an invisible source

But in the double seat in the back row
they only had eyes for each other

And I realised, looking down on them
I am a demi-god, I can turn out the light

I should have had the confidence
to focus on the beam from the projector
that illuminates
and the solid block of sound

I should have had an overall plan of more substance than simply
one reel after the other
or flicking between the channels

I should have stuck to the programme
things fall apart
sat in the double seat at the back of the picture house
they could have said
never write a word down unless you
know what the next word is going to be.

they could have said don't run away.
find your place, mark it out, defend it at all costs.

Fingers and Thumbs

Under the challenging light the man with no thumbs
was faced with a hand tool, matter more or less

intelligent and neither flesh nor bone a woman
with most of her fingers gone morrisons or in the skips

out the back where the free food is eager to please
I can see far out to sea. I can watch the sun set.

Or afternoons under the covers and between the
sheets a language read by index fingers placed

under one word after another spelling
out a meaning that is indistinct or hard to come by

Beach Head

for elisabeth

Below a certain size rock
becomes sand or other
ornamentation. Below a certain
size plastic particles become

indistinguishable from sand.
Breached below the waterline
the shore becomes a container
for anything that might be lost,

a clutch bag for the
ornaments the world
discards, a necklace of rare
plastic objects to adorn its

skin or the dusting of
light that sparkles from
the surface scratched away
through exposure to salt water

and inorganic to the last. A
chair to stare out to sea
and watch the beach slowly
piling up into unidentified

particles of plastic nets and
the debris from the fishing left

as lace to hang from
the shoulder of a cliff

or an arm stuck out
across the sea or spit
of land between your eyes
with no way to disentangle

sand from plastic or
the ornamental. Sand
drifting; in the middle
of the ocean

a plastic lake, the
items rubbing up
against each other small
yellow ducks bobbing.

Things come together
then disintegrate. Things
are full of dread,
the world, in its best dress.

Remarkable

1.
From cognac
To corn liquor
The headache
Remains the same

Footprints in the snow
Heavy paw marks
On the sphagnum
An indentation or

Nasty cough carried over
Into little addiction
Cilia's usual irritation
The plump armchair

Of shared genes
And the familiarity
Of the remarkable stroked
Against the fur surprised

His hair stood on end
Her's fell like a rope
Entwined in the flow, toe hold
Loose in the gravel bed

Some things may appear normal
Today it is sunny
Yesterday the sea was high
Tomorrow it may rain

2.
This is normal here
Where through clear air
The present sun
Bedazzled

Walking into the daylight
Shade don't last for ever
Sunlight on the
Edges of objects

The last silver leaves
Like a fringe on the
Top of a tree
Catching the light the

Mersea stone a throw
Away and a discarded
Oyster unpredictably
Twisted shiny shell

Remarkable
Characteristics
Patterns of
Increasing wealth

Workers on Point
Clear the waterside
Apartments where the
Tide usually goes

So from ferry travel, easy
Jet, a dog on a lead
Making tracks
Where mud remakes

Its own surface
How a boat makes way
As the water folds
Over itself how I step

Aside and haul
On the dog's
Chain or the way
Usual air passing

Will normally ruffle the
Tops of trees
Your hair moving
In the wind

3.
Falling for that old
Empire rope tick again

Power asserted
Over low lying land

The final touch
At the end of her fingers

Clicking where
Her family came to an end

Expression of hybrid vigour
Breeds coming together

Unfamiliar, energetic, remarkable

Norfolk

1.

Through the sand layer chalk appeared
embedded lines of flints like skulls thigh bones
after the ozone's gone the rainbow

And its doubled back indigo
a pale shadow and all the while

The flapping sound of clay
peeling off the mud cliffs

2.

The day is never normal
like flood or fire, light or dark
hailstones hitting my head
or peering through the windscreen
at the grey sky.

And in the day that is
never normal
the sea is never still
between defences.
Debris of beach huts,
the miniature lives
the small people
the shrinking rainbow
the cliffs wearing away. Nothing

remains the same and the clay
unfolding onto itself
the remains of a
big house tumbling.

A road leads over a cliff.
The sea milky after running over
exposed chalk with its fractured flint
skeletons a fossil appeared,
touching and touched back. The soft clay
rocks imitating granite as if the
world is now a play dough world that
can be manipulated.

3.

The distant mist
chalk dissolving
into air
falling in clouds.

And the cliff's double entry
waves washing at its feet
streams insinuating themselves.

Blackwater

Frozen in neutral under a hail of
Bullets. Flee and face certain death

Or remain and take your chances
With the blackwater firing squad

Holding the line of security up the
Muddy street the shooting

Lasting ten minutes maybe
Fifteen and Ali dead, a son, cousin

Unable to duck and his father
To take protective action.

The familiar figure holed and letting
Air out and blood under pressure

Thicker than the ebb and flow of the
Frozen blackwater supporting supply

And demand and oil of course thick
On the surface obscuring vision

Slipping into light, life leaking away
On the seat of his car and Ali

Unambivalent, neutralised and dead
To the world, disengaged and out of

Action. His father slipping the car into
First gear and driving nowhere the

Surface of the road frozen the surface
Beginning to thaw small waves

Emerged of anger and recrimination.
The law performs itself under inter-

National immunity, constructing
New ways for old, bullets through

The flesh of his flesh the car making
Circles in the road slowly as if there was

No one at the wheel tears falling like
Blood and dripping like water, thawing

Thick with history

Places too thick with history
To walk through a pea
Souper of the past the things

Unable to contain themselves
Or the bloody orders of
Induction and caesarean.

Places thinned out and hardly
There at all. This is where I was without
And here and on the other hand, all

Fingers spread to make a single span
Rivers renewing themselves
Seas washing in and out

Mud frozen into thin peaks
It's an ill wind, thin and biting flecks across
His iris small sparks from the past

I came and I saw this and this
I touched here and there I placed
Myself in this position, and then

The People Poems

Standing, watching

a girl standing watching a man washing his car arms folded a girl
watching a man

standing
laughing

the girl didn't have to be there the man didn't have to wash his car
they wanted to be there the girl standing laughing watching the man

standing over the car younger standing laughing her proud of him,
him of the car and her watching both proud pleased to be there
under the cliff face under the arched lintel

over their heads

trees grow from the ruins
under the cliff face a lintel
under the lintel a fireplace

standing laughing the boy and girl standing the car clean the clumps
of moss on the cliff face
like pillows lying laughing extracting water washing

He moved mountains

On the steep bank deeply churned by heavy machinery
One back leg braced against the slope
The front leg bent for stability
The man and the machine

Clumps of ladder ferns
Between the broken surfaces
Of the soil

Recently exposed rock

Men and their ways of standing
Their relationship to equipment
The jobs they will tackle
The earth they will move

People 5

Not bodies but the people in them
Turning and waving
Not the surface of the skin
But how it is
Under her skin

The miracle of life
Did I just say that
Time to breathe
To feel the little impulses
Movements towards

Trauma Unit
(Whiston Hospital)

Three men stand around a handbag, loose limbed
In the waiting room they waiting
The pink handbag soft and formless
Sequinned lying on the floor one man
Leans against a wall one leg bent the other
Straight a mobile phone in his hands
One man leans against a table both legs straight
Out in front of him one man stands
Unsupported, older, hitched over slightly and
All of them still, no nerves no jitters

The woman returns, picks up the handbag
Slings it over one shoulder in a single gesture
Embraces the older man the younger men move
Off the wall the table stand up straight
The group galvanised a young girl
Her arm supported by a pillow a
Young man pushed to the head of the queue

Flesh and blood
The women move off the older man stands
Holding the handbag, still, one man
His body hitched to one side an older man
A pink handbag held straight by his sides
Standing still

On a station

Cleaning the far end of the platform
Beyond where the people went
Grimacing to himself
His foot extended like a dancer
In a perfect point
Rubbing at the ground in front of him
Loosening gum
Arms out like a cormorant drying on a rock
Maintaining balance

People 8

It wasn't so much your appearance
But how you looked
Stepping out of the shadows
Agitated and partially formed

Each tilted plane of upturned nose of
Cheek bone held against the light
That shone from eyes that might
Reflect the compliment
Of every wink of all emotion

The Day the Hell's Angels Came to Brightlingsea

The day the Hell's Angels came to Brightlingsea
Nothing happened
I was drinking with Ralph in the corner behind the pool table and next to the fruit machine
Dave the landlord who fancied himself a bit even if no-one else did disappeared
And sent his wife Christine to clear them out

Which, in the end, she did

We sat against the wall
They performed centre stage
Andy came in with his dog, a kind of Doberman
And we always had Andy down as a bit of a bullshitter
Claimed to be a bodyguard to celebrities

As we sat, pinned against the wall, Andy moved through them
Easily with no trace of anxiety
Like a knife through hot butter
The hardened denim and leather
Resistant to any fold
Let him pass

Andy did time for rape later. Ralph
Ducks his head when he sees him coming

Anyway the Angels began to misbehave, a little self-consciously
Christine threw them out
They did nothing, moving towards the door

We moved to the middle of the pub past the pool table
Away from the windows
Expecting bricks
Hearing the engines start up
Already seeing the flying glass
Nothing happened

Shop Talk

After assessing chip shops
They spoke of the Chinese.

The white man on a bar stool speaking loudly
Says they gamble
Even on the speed of drops of water
Down a window pane,
That they don't eat from their own takeaways.

We sat some distance away and ate crisps
When two women entered
Thin elderly women as if from the National Trust.
Do you do food they asked and where do we eat.

The pub fell silent. These women were
Stranger than the Chinese,
Or the Indians who invented Tikka Masala,
These women with their uncertainty about food in
The small bar or the company they might keep.

An announcement

A train and its people on it
No-one at the controls
Pieces of flesh
On rails
Little point less direction

People not machines
Gathering in dark matter
Pooling beneath the surface
In the hidden depths
Pressure points

Out of reach
Pleasing a distant
Or long dead father
Holding up the service
For an announcement

Thank you father
For what sustains us
We are small in stature
Next to steel work
We are soft in the head

Exhausted from metal
Fatigue and the stress
Fractures pitting ourselves
In the fabrication
Of the surface

People Again

So much appearance and the way you
Looked you agitated shadows
Stiffening in resolve and partly formed
Each tilted plane of upturned nose of
Cheek bone held against the light
That shone from eyes that might
Reflect the compliment
Of every wink of all emotion

Just sixteen and marriage on the cards
You smoke weed? she asked and why not
Like those that take up space as if they own it
And when I thought I'd said goodbye
When I thought I'd said some other thing
I'd said that again that counts for nothing
That you can depend on and can count on
Me for every 1,2,3

I wonder, idly, what the small life might be like
How it might fill up lonely hours
Never having been in the wilds
Brisk people and the bodies in them
Standing awkwardly performing to a format

The Scale of Love

Splashing in water set to the exact temperature
Of the human body I can hardly
Feel myself under these conditions

The scale is oceanic
A lost soul pining for a lost soul
Trackless seas
I entertained my self

As best I could
Under such conditions
Of unfamiliarity
And in the setting aside of duty

Is this what I want?
The orchestration of starlings
Coming home to roost.
The road becomes a four lane highway, no

An eight lane highway no the road becomes
A trackless ocean no the road becomes
The principle of division and a gap
Between the language of love

The body of all knowledge
And its application and
Drops of water drying on hot skin
Magnified out of all proportion

www.ingramcontent.com/pod-product-compliance
Lightning Source LLC
Chambersburg PA
CBHW031158160426
43193CB00008B/429